# The Hepworth Wakefield

ART SPACES

## INTRODUCTION

The Hepworth Wakefield is the UK's major new art gallery, designed by award-winning British architect, Sir David Chipperfield. It is a highly sculptural building constructed in pigmented cast concrete and situated at the heart of Wakefield's historic waterfront on the River Calder, so that it appears to dip its toes in the fast-flowing river.

The gallery celebrates and explores the region's heritage as the birthplace of modern British sculpture through the achievements of Barbara Hepworth (1903–75) and Henry Moore (1898–1986) – two of the most important artists of the twentieth century, both of whom were born and grew up in the Wakefield district. It was the landscape and industry in the old West Riding of Yorkshire that provided valuable early experiences for these two extraordinary sculptors and now create a fertile context for our collection displays and temporary exhibitions programme.

The Hepworth Wakefield offers audiences access to world-class art and a new home for Wakefield's major art collection, which was founded in 1923. We provide opportunities for international artists to have large-scale exhibitions in a rich art historical context, and through strategic partnerships with Tate, the Arts Council Collection and the British Council we also ensure that work from national collections is shown regularly in Yorkshire.

At the heart of the gallery are two locally born artists – Hepworth and Moore – who forged international reputations while drawing creatively on their Yorkshire backgrounds. Both artists continue to inspire new generations, and we celebrate and explore their legacy by examining the spirit of

→ The Hepworth Wake from the footbridge, 2011

ce in Yorkshire while fostering new international
nnections. Our collection contains iconic works by
pworth, Moore and their contemporaries, housed
a state-of-the-art building that is one of the largest
pose-built galleries in the UK.

From an early age, Hepworth was interested in
power of architecture, particularly as her father
s a surveyor to the West Riding of Yorkshire. She
en accompanied him as he travelled through the
unty, one that is rich in inspirational landscapes
h many sculptural qualities such as hollows,
aks, rolling hills, dry-stone walls and impressive
ggy outcrops. It is a terrain in which man has
o made his mark through mining, creating deep
fts and slag and spoil heaps in extracting the
v materials of coal and lead ore. Hepworth often
trasted the natural beauty she found in Yorkshire
h 'the unnatural', as she put it, 'disorder of
towns, the slag heaps, the dirt and ugliness.'
rbara Hepworth: Retrospective Exhibition 1927–
54, Whitechapel Art Gallery, London, 1954.)
Hepworth, of course, associated closely with
sts and architects as friends and colleagues.

← Barbara Hepworth,
*Pierced Hemisphere I*,
1937
↓ Henry Moore,
*Reclining Figure*, 1936

In *Unit One*, an avant-garde group formed by Paul Nash in 1933, artists from the modern movement, including Hepworth, Tristram Hillier, Moore, Ben Nicholson and Edward Wadsworth, came together with architects Colin Lucas and Wells Coates. Hepworth knew Walter Gropius from when they both lived in Hampstead after he fled Germany, and she and Nicholson were also befriended by the architects Leslie Martin and his wife Sadie Speight.

During 1936–7, they all jointly compiled material that formed the basis of the publication *Circle, an international survey of Constructive Art* edited by Nicholson, Martin and Naum Gabo. Under four headings – 'Painting', 'Sculpture', 'Architecture', and 'Art and Life' – the editors of *Circle* brought together what they called 'forces which seem to us to be working in the same direction and for the same ideas.' *Circle* emphasised the cross-pollination of disciplines and a new internationalism and idealism in which Hepworth participated. This has a fascinating relationship to the globalised and digitally converged world in which we now live.

The Hepworth Wakefield draws on and furthers this dialogue between art and architecture, and is a major addition to the visual arts infrastructure in the UK. Its spacious, light-filled galleries attract artists of international standing to exhibit as part of our ambitious contemporary programme, along with emerging artists who have the opportunity to present career-defining exhibitions. The Hepworth Wakefield's exhibition programme makes valuable connections between historic and contemporary art,

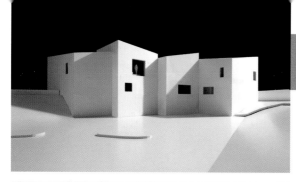

← Architect's model, from the river, 2007
→ Gallery 6 – Hepworth and St Ives, 2011

← David Chipperfield Architects' Competition Sketch, 2003

challenging perceptions and encouraging debate through its research and Learning Programme. Ma of our exhibitions support the creation of new wor produced in response to the gallery's architecture, collection and its unique locality.

In designing The Hepworth Wakefield, David Chipperfield Architects reacted imaginatively to the gallery's dramatic waterfront setting, which features a new pedestrian bridge alongside the existing road bridge and weir. The building complements the scale and form of the existing industrial buildings and like them appears to rise out of the River Calder. The gallery's location on the river's edge also allows it to exploit new forms of renewable energy by making use of the river's flow as part of the cooling system. It takes full advantage of its site allowing both the interior and exterior to have a mutually enhancing relationship.

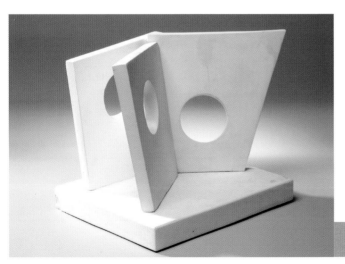

← Barbara Hepworth, *Three Oblique Forms*, 1967

David Chipperfield
Architects' Concept
Image, 2003
Gallery 3 – Hepworth in
Context, 2011

The gallery's smooth concrete exterior is pigmented to give it a faint purplish-grey hue called Hepworth Brown. This mutable façade and the skewed angular forms give the building its sculptural appearance, which echoes the clarity and power in Barbara Hepworth's works. There is a sympathetic relationship between the forms and volumes that Chipperfield created for the gallery and those used by Hepworth in works such as *Six Forms on a Circle* (1967), *Three Oblique Forms* (1967), *Six Forms (2x3)* (1968) and *Conversation with Magic Stones* (1973). It is revealing that one of Chipperfield's models for the building was actually carved out of a single piece of limestone to create a chiselled solid object – Hepworth would certainly have approved of its rigour, sensibility and plain speaking.

The Hepworth Wakefield's interior has, alongside the collection galleries, 650 square metres for temporary exhibitions, making it one of the largest contemporary exhibition spaces outside London. The design of the galleries allows the introduction of daylight through skylights and impressive floor-to-ceiling windows. These windows offer visitors wonderful views of the River Calder and important local landmarks such as the medieval Chantry Chapel and Wakefield Cathedral. The natural light that enters the gallery plays a crucial role in creating a highly sympathetic environment in which to have an aesthetic experience. Each of the galleries has its own character and atmosphere while never forgetting that the central reason for its design is to display works of art to their best advantage.

One of the great successes and pleasures of the building is the way in which the sequence of 10 gallery spaces unfolds for the visitor, following a dynamic, flowing route that encourages connections to be made between works of art. The internal volumes allow both a sense of grandeur and domesticity created by the variable pitch of the ceiling in each room. This provides a captivating balance for visitors, so that each space is a surprise and not merely another uniform, featureless box, all too common in gallery design. The visitor is offered fascinating views and glimpses from gallery to gallery, so that the building feels more than the sum of its parts. It encourages people to linger, pause,

The gallery at night, 2011

retrace steps and enjoy the contingency of changing light conditions on the works of art.

The Hepworth Wakefield take its place amongst David Chipperfield Architects' internationally distinguished portfolio of projects and will be enjoyed for generations to come as a place to experience the power and inspiration of great art and architecture. It is a wonderful gallery in which to curate art collections and exhibition programmes, and a crucial place to visit regularly.

Simon Wallis
*Director*

## BUILDING THE HEPWORTH WAKEFIELD

In embarking on The Hepworth Wakefield project and launching the international competition to select the architect in 2003, Wakefield Council declared that it wanted to create an 'exceptionally high quality and inspiring building which will become synonymous with the City of Wakefield' (Architects' Brief, 2003). The brief talked of the completed art gallery being of international significance and a landmark building. Eight years later, with the opening of The Hepworth Wakefield in May 2011, it is clear from the public and critical response that Chipperfield's design and the quality of the curatorship more than meet the ambitions for the project.

The origins of the project go back well before 2003. The old City Council opened Wakefield Art Gallery in 1934 in a solid and attractive 1880s house on Wentworth Terrace after carrying out limited works to convert it from a home into a gallery. As early as 1938, the first Director, Ernest Musgrave, wrote:

> The collections in all sections have been doubled during the last four years and it is impossible to arrange the permanent collections in their entirety in the space available. It cannot be denied that the popularity of the gallery alone justifies an extension of premises for there is no doubt that it is regarded as one of the most progressive galleries in the provinces. (Report to Wakefield City Council, July 1938.)

The start of the Second World War cut short any plans and the gallery remained in its old home and without any extension until it closed and the collection

→ The Hepworth Wakefi
under construction,
2008

← Aerial photograph of waterfront site, 1933

was transferred to The Hepworth Wakefield Trust in 2009 as custodians on behalf of Wakefield Council.

By the early 1990s, the many weaknesses of the old gallery were increasingly apparent: it was sited well away from the city centre, was inaccessible and lacked facilities for learning and study, had no café or shop, and had space to display only about five per cent of the works in the collection. The domestic scale of the display space limited the ambition of the temporary exhibition programme and the scale of work that could be accommodated.

The limitations were reflected in declining attendances and the gallery no longer enjoyed the reputation for having an exciting and pioneering programme as it had done in the first 25 years when the Directors both exhibited and acquired important contemporary work. It was many years since *The Guardian* newspaper had written, when Helen Kapp was Director in the 1950s, that 'although one of the smallest and newest of the provincial galleries, Wakefield is able year after year to mount exhibitions of contemporary art which easily surpass

terest what the provinces usually have to offer.'
ntemporary Art at Wakefield', *The Guardian*,
September 1956.)

Although, at this early stage, the size, nature
location of the gallery remained undefined,
concept of a new contemporary art gallery for
efield, with the collection at the heart of the
s, gained increasing credibility and momentum.
vital elements transformed the project from
mple re-housing of the existing collection.
se were the offer to the City of Wakefield, made
he Trustees of the Barbara Hepworth Estate in
7, of the gift of 'the collection of twenty plus
nal plaster sculptures that remained in the
io of Dame Barbara Hepworth at the time
er death' and the growing recognition of the
orical significance of Wakefield's waterfront
the opportunities to develop it as a catalyst for
city's regeneration. There was also increasing
reness of the cultural significance of Yorkshire
he birthplace of modern British sculpture
the influence of the landscape within striking
ance of Wakefield and Castleford on the

→ Barbara Hepworth
working on *Curved
Form (Bryher II)*, Palais
de Danse, 1961

formative years of two of the century's greatest sculptors, Moore and Hepworth. As the project developed, these initial strengths were extended and expanded most spectacularly through the exceptional quality of Chipperfield's architecture and the gallery's curatorship, the excellence of the opening programme and the support of key partners including Tate, the Arts Council Collection and many private lenders.

The journey from the initial concept to completion was eventful and lengthy. The letter of 2 October 1997 from Sir Alan Bowness, for the Trustees of the Hepworth Estate, offering the gift of Hepworth's original plaster sculptures set the city a challenge 'that a building of architectural distinction and museum standard would be made available' for the gift. This added weight to the objective of matching the quality of the gallery's collection with the architecture, and to make it an ambitious project that would deliver significant cultural and regeneration benefits for Wakefield and Yorkshire.

To promote the project to potential partners and develop strategic support, Wakefield Council,

working with the newly-formed Waterfront Partnership, published the proposal for the new art gallery in 1997. In February 1999, the Council produced the Strategic Brief, prepared by Wakefield Art Gallery with the Council's Regeneration Service. This document set the defining characteristics of the new gallery and made the case for support. Much of the thinking informed the final brief issued as part of the later architectural competition.

By 2000, formal feasibility studies for the gallery and the Waterfront development demonstrated the strength of the proposal and that placing it within the Waterfront would provide both a stimulating setting for the gallery and give the wider development a national and international profile. A key element of the business case was that The Hepworth Wakefield would add to the critical mass of visual arts venues within a 10-mile radius: the highly successful Yorkshire Sculpture Park, which started at West Bretton in 1977 and was already developing the new visitor centre, which opened in 2002, and planning the underground galleries, which were completed in 2005; the Henry Moore Institute, which opened to great acclaim in Leeds in 1993; and Leeds Art Gallery, which had origins going back to the nineteenth century.

Despite being sure of the considerable benefits of the new art gallery, commencement of project development and delivery was delayed until 2003. This was the result of the lengthy process of assembling the land to enable the preferred developer, CTP St James, to commission a

← Barbara Hepworth, *The Family of Man*, 1 Yorkshire Sculpture F
→ Wakefield Waterfront image created for the developer, CTP St Ja

comprehensive masterplan, and the complexity of developing a brownfield site within a former industrial area. A fundamental issue was finalising the location of the gallery within the Waterfront. Early discussions centred around restoring and extending the Calder and Hebble Navigation Warehouse, a fine 1790s stone building, but by 2001 it was clear that the commercial considerations of the building's owners, British Waterways, and the constraints associated with converting a listed building into a modern art gallery would make this impractical. Instead, the more prominent and open site at the north end of the Waterfront offered a much more interesting location that would give the architect the opportunity to create a new building in an exciting position beside the river. This derelict site was within the Waterfront Conservation Area with the navigation to the west and the fast-flowing river running over the weir to the north. It was close to the medieval Chantry Bridge and Chapel at Wakefield's main river crossing, which was a popular subject for artists including J.M.W. Turner (1775–1851), who

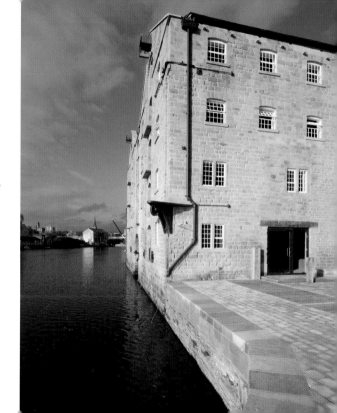

The international architectural competition, run with the Royal Institute of British Architects, was launched in May 2003. The brief for the competition, though based on the earlier strategic brief, reflected the consultation with local people, artists and key partners. The competition attracted an impressive 111 expressions of interest and the Jury Panel selected a strong shortlist to develop concept designs. The six architects, David Adjaye, David Chipperfield, Zaha Hadid, Kengo Kuma, Snohetta and Spence, and Walters and Cohen produced very different designs and approaches to the site. The Panel unanimously selected David Chipperfield Architects and they were announced as winners in November 2003.

David Chipperfield Architects' competition concept and supporting statement stressed the importance of scale, light and the sequence of spaces, all key elements of the completed gallery. There is clear continuity between the concept images of top-lit galleries with sloping ceilings and the finished building; and the proposal that 'the walls of the gallery building will form a positive edge –

painted it in 1797–98. There was an interesting group of eighteenth and nineteenth-century warehouse and mill buildings to the south of the site. These were built when Wakefield was a thriving inland port at the junction of the Aire and Calder Navigation, which linked Wakefield with the sea, and the Calder and Hebble Navigation, which led into the Pennines and routes to Manchester.

reinforcing the winding edge of the river' was carri[ed]
through to completion. The accompanying stateme[nt]
noted '… the exhibition spaces will respond to the
objects that are within it – creating spaces with
sculptural qualities and overriding neutrality, withou[t]
becoming sculptures themselves.' On describing
the sequence of spaces, Chipperfield wrote 'the
gallery should naturally and enjoyably lead the visi[tor]
through a sequence of "rooms"…this sequence
of spaces should allow the visitor to select a route
enjoying a series of views, varying spaces and
daylight conditions, encouraging the visitor to be l[ed]
from one room to another.' The architects viewed [the]
open site as an opportunity to have all the exhibiti[on]
galleries on one level, terming this 'The Horizontal
Gallery', which 'allows all galleries to have the
potential to connect to the exterior landscape' with
the possibility of top-lit galleries: 'Light is a materi[al]
of a museum. Its manipulation is fundamental to th[e]
nature of a gallery.' (David Chipperfield Architects'
entry to the RIBA Competition, September 2003.)

With the successful outcome of the competiti[on]
and through other appointments, the Council

sembled the highly skilled design team to take the complexities and challenges of designing d delivering The Hepworth Wakefield. As well as vid Chipperfield Architects as lead designers, the ject team included Ramboll as structural and chanical and electrical engineers; Arup as lighting d security consultants; Gross Max landscape signers; and Turner and Townsend as project d cost managers. The design team started in oruary 2004 with a series of workshops to test e brief with the small client team and establish ared understanding of the project objectives and proach to the site. The design process involved rking closely with the Hepworth Estate and study is with the architects, including visits to see the pworth plasters in St Ives, Chipperfield's newly mpleted Figge Gallery in Davenport, Iowa, and view both gallery design and use of concrete, rticularly as a façade material, in Switzerland, chtenstein and Austria.

There were key points in the project development it progressed through the design development ges to the appointment of the contractor,

← David Chipperfield
leading a tour,
April 2011
→ David Chipperfield
Architects' Competition
Sketches, 2003

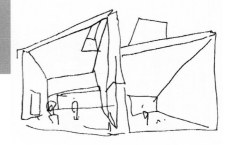

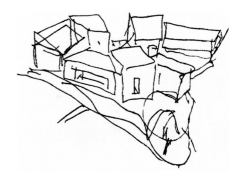

ng O'Rourke, and start of construction in 2007.
nnecting the gallery to the city centre was an early
ue, for the site lies at the southern extremity of
 centre and beside a main north–south roadway.
create a direct link over the river to the city and
move the entrance away from the busy road, the
uncil added a new pedestrian bridge to the project
ing 2004. The Waterfront masterplan, prepared
Faulkner Browns, had proposed two footbridges
ated further south, but these depended on
mpletion of the associated developments.
ocating the footbridge to the north meant that
ould be integrated with the gallery and lead the
tor to the entrance to the building, the garden
 the waterfront. It also delivered the practical
nefit that the gallery car park could be placed
 the north side of the river, freeing up space for
velopment to the south.

The Commission for Architecture and the
lt Environment (CABE) reviewed the Waterfront
sterplan and Chipperfield's designs for the gallery
2004. The latter was at the start of the detailed
sign stage and was an influential confirmation of

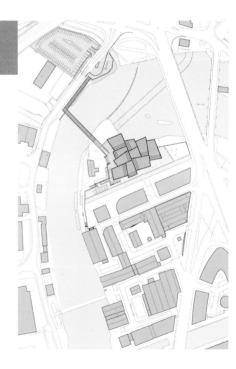

← David Chipperfield
Architects' Concept
Images, 2007
→ Site plan, 2007

the strength of Chipperfield's concept. Integral to this was endorsement of the quality of the galleries and that designing all of these to the same standard would create the necessary flexibility to display the existing collection of painting and sculpture, the gift from the Hepworth Estate, which by then had increased to 40 works, tools and other material from Hepworth's studio, and future loans and exhibitions. In 2005, CABE featured the building in *Design Reviewed*, its annual review, impressed by 'its strong diagram of individual volumetric forms, which are expressed both at ground and first-floor levels.' (CABE, *Design Reviewed* 2, March 2005.)

Over the course of the project, the design went through a number of iterations to reach the final form. This was a complex process in which the architects involved and challenged the client team. As Chipperfield noted shortly before the gallery opened:

Interestingly, we did have to adopt a conventional sculptural technique of composition to get to the final design. We made perhaps a hundred models to work out what size things should be, and to get enough difference between one roof corner and another, and to make the building work inside. Obviously if you push one corner down, then another has to come up … If you strike a line across it, it is basically a flat building. There's only about a 1.5 metre variation between one corner and the other … There was the question of how big the separate volumes should be. We could have made them smaller, but as soon as you make them smaller, then all of a sudden it doesn't look very satisfactory from a sculptural point of view. We had versions where there were twenty-four separate volumes, and we had some where there were five volumes. That manipulation was a very sculptural process.*

Fundraising ran in parallel with project development and the first significant external funding came in

*Unless stated otherwise, all quotations by David Chipperfield are taken from an interview with Sarah Wedderburn on 18 April 2011, commissioned by The Hepworth Wakefield.

February 2004, when Arts Council England awarded their maximum grant of £5 million. This was followed with a grant for a similar sum from the Heritage Lottery Fund, and other major grants from Yorkshire Forward, the Homes and Communities Agency, and the European Regional Development Fund, as well as a number of trusts and foundations. All of these were matched with Council capital.

The project's greatest challenge came when it went out to tender for the contractor in 2006 at a time when there was a very buoyant market. The tenders returned in August were significantly over budget. Undaunted, the project team started value engineering with the contractor, Laing O'Rourke, and this resulted nearly a year later in an affordable main contract; the building was 10 per cent smaller but retained all the qualities of the original design. In the process, some of the fundamental aspects of the design were questioned. As Chipperfield recalled in 2011, the building's relationship with the site and the river had to be defended through this process:

In Wakefield I think it was the idea of trying to create something that had a certain authority that would plant itself as if it couldn't be anywhere else than there. So making the river form the edge was critical. That was a big thing to fight for, because technically it was difficult. We had to spend money on that, and in the value engineering that the project went through, it was always under threat, but I thought it was important. If you go round the corner you see the 19th century buildings and they go straight into the water, like sort of Venetian palazzos.

Laing O'Rourke took on the challenges of the project and, despite difficulties with flooding and contamination, the building was completed and handed over in January 2010. The contractors cast all of the walls of the building on site using pigmented, self-compacting concrete to create a glorious sculptural façade that is smooth to the touch, dynamically reflects the changing light and delivers Chipperfield's concept: 'the external volume expresses internal space … So there is a continuous

→ Constructing the galle first floor, 2009

dialogue in this project between the spaces that the external shapes form, and the form that the internal spaces generate'.

In 2011, Chipperfield's response to the observation that the building is more than the sum of its parts and that it has a kind of energy about it, was an interesting insight into designing The Hepworth Wakefield:

If you get a good concept, then it's a matter of trying to find what that idea wants to be and how best to fulfil it. And then if you follow it in a good way, it nearly tells you what to do. It's about listening to what it wants to do. Certain projects, once they're off and running, you've just got to let it roll. And some buildings are better than others at telling you what to do. The idea may be not strong enough to do it. Clearly here it kept telling you what to do, and therefore you get something where everything has to re-form each other. In this case, the internal composition of space had to inform the external volumetric composition. The external composition had to keep re-informing the internal. And how you build that – where you put the skylights, where you put the windows, the circulation – it all starts to become dynamic. It's like taking a machine apart. In a good building all the bits have somehow been rattled around till nothing… Michelangelo said that to find the essence of a sculpture you roll it down a mountain. Whatever's left is the sculpture, and I think that's true about architecture, or any sort of composition. You want to roll it so all the loose bits have fallen off, and nothing is superfluous.

Gordon Watson
*Chief Executive, Lakeland Arts Trust*

Gordon Watson was Project Director at The Hepworth Wakefield from 2004 to 2010 and was previously Manager of Wakefield Council's Museum and Arts Service.

## THE WAKEFIELD ART COLLECTION

Only five years after its opening in 1934 on Wentworth Terrace, the Director of Wakefield Art Gallery was able to report that the gallery was building a 'comprehensive collection of contemporary art' and that it was becoming 'one of the most progressive galleries in the provinces.' (Director's Report, 1939.) Founded initially in 1923 with gifts of mostly historic art from local industrialists, the gallery went on to support and collect works by some of the most significant and avant-garde British artists of the twentieth century. Through the influence of pioneering Directors such as Musgrave, Eric Westbrook and Helen Kapp, who worked at Wakefield Art Gallery between the 1930s and the 1950s, the gallery's remarkable commitment to contemporary art is evident in works by artists including locally born Hepworth

← Wakefield Art Gallery

→ Barbara Hepworth, *Two Forms with White (Greek)*, 1963; and Henry Moore, *Head of a Woman*, 1926

and Moore, alongside others such as Ivon Hitchens (1893–1979), Ben Nicholson (1894–1982), John Piper (1903–92) and Victor Pasmore (1908–98).

To showcase the twentieth-century content of the Wakefield art collection and to provide a context for the gift of plasters from the Hepworth Estate, the opening year's collection displays highlighted Hepworth's significance. With the addition of key loans from the national collections held at Tate, the Arts Council, the British Council, as well as other organisations and private lenders, the displays presented a cohesive narrative illustrating the many facets of Hepworth's career in the context of her national and international contemporaries.

The visitor first encountered Hepworth's sculpture in Gallery 1, in a display that explored the extraordinary breadth and quality of her work with five sculptures foregrounding the strong connection between material, method and subject matter. The pierced and stringed cast bronze of *Spring* (1966) breaks open the solid object and activates it with colour. The upright carved form of *Figure (Nanjizal)* (1958) retains a clear relationship to the original form of the tree trunk and the landscape. *Cosdon Head* (1949) uses carved lines to lightly describe the contours of a hand against the face. The formal clarity of *Cone and Sphere* (1973) brings together abstraction with an allusion to the upright body, and *Two Forms with White (Greek)* (1963) presents figure and object in conversation with each other.

Gallery 2 reflected on the legacy of Wakefield Art Gallery and featured works acquired for the collection by some of the early pioneering Directors and the innovative exhibitions that gave the gallery a national reputation. The works on display also indicated the support received by the gallery from organisations such as the Contemporary Art Society, the Art Fund, the V&A Purchase Grant Fund as well as private donors and the subscribers to the Wakefield Permanent Art Fund, all of whom supported the purchase of contemporary works. Highlights included works by Camden Town artists Harold Gilman (1876–1919) and Spencer Gore (1878–1914), as well as Moore's *Head of a Woman* (1926) and Patrick Heron's (1920–99) *St Ives Churchyard* (1950).

→ Barbara Hepworth, *Mother and Child*, 1934

In Gallery 3, the display explored the work of Hepworth in relation to her European contemporaries and focused on the influence of direct carving on Modern British sculpture. Her changing ideas about sculpture, like many other British artists, were influenced by an awareness of artistic developments on the Continent and an increased interest in sculpture and objects from across the globe. An earlier generation of sculptors, including Constantin Brancusi (1876–1957), Jacob Epstein (1880–1959) and Henri Gaudier-Brzeska (1891–1915), had already broken away from the tradition of modelling and classical representation. They explored new possibilities offered through direct carving, a principle of truth to materials whereby the sculpture's form was dictated by the shape, density and the integral markings of wood grain or stone.

The spirit of international artistic exchange was sustained through visits by British artists to Paris and the subsequent exile of many members of the European avant-garde seeking refuge from the Nazi occupation. Piet Mondrian (1872–1944) and Naum Gabo (1890–1977) based themselves in London

← Barbara Hepworth,
*Curved Forms (Pavan)*,
1956 (plaster)

→ Barbara Hepworth,
*Pelagos*, 1946;
and far right Barbara
Hepworth, *White Core*
1955–6/1960 (plaste

in the late 1930s, where Continental Modernism intersected with a British sensibility towards the landscape and the figure. This resulted in a stylistic change in British painting and sculpture from the literal description of the subject to a concentration on simplified form and abstraction.

Galleries 4 and 5 house permanent displays based around the gift from the Hepworth Estate. Hepworth at Work explores Hepworth's studio environment, her working practice in plaster, her collaborative relationships with bronze foundries, and the monumental commissions she received in the last 15 years of her life. The tools and materials on display here were Hepworth's own and have been drawn from her second studio in St Ives, the Palais de Danse. Also featured is a step-by-step reconstruction of the bronze-casting process, photographs of works in progress and four specially commissioned films containing archival footage of the artist in her studio.

The display introduces the Hepworth Family Gift, a remarkable collection of Hepworth's surviving working models for her bronze sculptures, the

jority of which were made in plaster. This
nerous gift was made by the Hepworth Family
ough the Art Fund and was one of the key
sons for building a new gallery for Wakefield,
nnecting Hepworth's name with the city in which
e was born and grew up.

The collection reflects the variety of ways in
ich Hepworth used plaster and aluminium as
t of her working process. She preferred to
ke prototypes on the same scale as the finished
lptures and would have worked directly on the
jority of these models. The centrepiece of the
t is the aluminium prototype for *Winged Figure*
)61–63), the sculpture commissioned by John
wis for its flagship store on Oxford Street, London.
nearly 6 metres high, this is the only working
del to survive from the monumental commissions
pworth received in later life.

Although Hepworth's formative years were
ent in Wakefield, her later years in Cornwall have
ulted in the artist's close association with the
n of St Ives. In Gallery 6, the display explored
Cornish town's history as an artists' colony

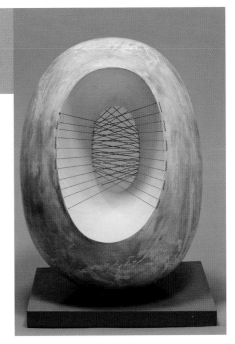

← Hepworth's sculpture as
seen in the Palais de
Danse, 1961; and below
Gallery 4 – Hepworth
at Work, 2011
→ Barbara Hepworth
*Spring*, 1966 (plaster)

dating from the late nineteenth century. Just before the outbreak of the Second World War, Hepworth left London with Nicholson and their triplets for the safety of St Ives. They found themselves within an active artistic community, which included the ceramicists Bernard Leach (1887–1979) and, later, his wife Janet (1918–97), the art theorist and artist Adrian Stokes (1902–72) and his wife the artist Margaret Mellis (1914–2009), and the Cornish-born artist Peter Lanyon (1918–64). They were shortly followed by Naum and Miriam Gabo and subsequently many more artists were drawn to this small town. This combination of innovative artists and inspiring landscapes lead to the development of a particularly British abstraction and St Ives became an internationally significant centre for the development of post-war contemporary art.

Yorkshire in Pictures is a dedicated space in Gallery 6, which highlights another key aspect of Wakefield's collection, that of architectural and landscape works. This includes the Gott Collection, 10 volumes of images of eighteenth and nineteenth-century Yorkshire. This fascinating visual resource is

→ Gallery 5 – The
Hepworth Plasters, 2011

→ Patrick Heron,
*St Ives Churchyard,
night*, 1950

→ Richard Ramsay Reinagle,
*Ruins of the Duke of
York's Chapel, Wakefield
Bridge*, n.d.

accessible to view via a digital catalogue.
opening displays included J.M.W. Turner's
tch of Wakefield's Chantry Chapel on loan
n the British Museum, alongside a selection
aintings, drawings and prints of this historic
mark drawn from the Wakefield collection.
displays change on a regular basis to draw
other themes and also to include non-historic
ks and works by amateur artists produced as
sult of the Learning Programme.
The collection displays will change on a
ly basis as more works from the Wakefield
ection are brought out from store and the loans
gramme develops to reflect other themes in
sh twentieth-century art. Future displays will
us on the artists associated with the 'Geometry
ear', such as Moore, Reg Butler (1913–81) and
nard Meadows (1915–2005), and other themes
to be addressed will include twentieth-century
artists' concern with imagery of the mother and
child, and works depicting warfare. There will also
be exhibitions that examine particular works from
the collection in detail, for example, James Tissot's
(1836–1902) On the Thames (1876).

## THE TEMPORARY EXHIBITIONS PROGRAMME

The Hepworth Wakefield provides an extraordinary context for a programme of ambitious temporary exhibitions. The immediate architectural setting of Chipperfield's series of spatially unique galleries insists on a collaborative working process with contemporary artists. Their art must necessarily respond to shifts in scale (walls that double in height from one corner to another) and to the constantly changing experience of light in the galleries, which is subject to conditions outside, rather than within, the spaces. Furthermore, both the immediate and distant landscape are framed by each carefully considered window, explicitly connecting the experience of the interior of the Hepworth to both the nearby waterfront warehouses and the hills of the Yorkshire landscape. This emphasis on environment draws together contemporary Wakefield's post-industrial city status with a history of British landscape and modernist art, and it is through connections to both past and present that the exhibition programme will develop. As it was for Hepworth and Moore, the Yorkshire setting will provide a rich context for artistic collaboration and international ambition.

The inaugural exhibition, Eva Rothschild's *Hot Touch*, presented the work of one of the foremost international contemporary sculptors working in the UK. Rothschild (b.1972) makes her sculptures from a range of different materials including fabric, beads, polystyrene, leather and wood, crafted by hand and sometimes fabricated using industrial processes. This focus on making foregrounded not only the formal connections between her and Hepworth's sculpture (the modernist innovation of the hole punched through and opening up sculpture

→ Eva Rothschild, *Hot*
at The Hepworth Wak
21 May–9 October 2

resonates in Rothschild's explorations of space in and around her work) but also ideas of process that are so central to the display of prototypes and plasters in the Hepworth Family Gift. As the first artist to exhibit in the spaces, Rothschild exploited their variation, making sculptures that levitated in, and propped up the highest corners of the gallery, placed in relation to other works, such as the visual gravitational pull of a huge segmented, mosaic covered black doughnut. The subsequent exhibition, *The Unquiet Head* by Clare Woods (b.1972), presented vast paintings of a psychologically charged landscape. Future exhibitions will embrace and disturb these gallery spaces, drawing on The Hepworth Wakefield's art-historic collections as well as contemporary work.

Rothschild,
*n of Plenty*, 2011

Clare Woods,
*The Intended*, 2011
(detail)

← Eva Rothschild, *Hot Touch* at The Hepworth Wakefield
→ Eva Rothschild, *Sunrise*, 2011

## EXTERIOR WORKS

The gallery is set in a garden that follows the
contours of the River Calder and is bounded by
the brick warehouses to the south of the site.
For the gallery launch and the first year of opening,
Heather (b.1973) and Ivan Morison (b.1974)
were invited to reinstall their architectural sculpture
commissioned by Situations at the University
of the West of England in 2009. *The Black Cloud*
takes its shape from Amazonian dwellings used by
the Yanomamo tribe for performances, discussion
and play, and was built in the Amish tradition of
a barn-raising. It has been conceived to provide
protection from various imagined climatic scenarios
– the structure itself is protected from the elements
by an ancient Japanese wood-scorching technique –
and is a hybrid of both sculpture and multi-functional
social space.

↔ Heather and Ivan
Morison, *The Black
Cloud*, 2009, during
the opening weekend,
2011

Elsewhere in the gallery's grounds are further examples of Hepworth's bronze sculptures, both from the Wakefield art collection and on loan from the Hepworth Estate. Three figures from the series *The Family of Man* (1970) – *Parent I*, *Parent II* and *Young Girl* – are sited on the headland above the weir just before the entrance to the gallery. The garden in front of the watermill includes the bronze *Hollow Form with Inner Form* (1968). Inside the gallery, the plaster working model for this sculpture can be found amongst the Hepworth Family Gift.

At the rear of the gallery, in the east garden, there are two sculptures donated in 2011 from a private collection through the Contemporary Art Society. Another bronze by Hepworth, *Ascending Form (Gloria)* (1958), sits alongside a sculpture cast in aluminium by Hubert Dalwood (1914–76), *Minos* (1962).

Frances Guy
*Head of Collection and Exhibitions*

opening weekend, 2011

← The gallery at night, 2011, showing figures from *The Family of Man*, 1970, by Barbara Hepworth

© Scala Publishers Ltd, 2012
Text © The Hepworth Wakefield

First published in 2012 by
Scala Publishers Ltd
Northburgh House
10 Northburgh Street
London EC1V 0AT
Telephone: +44 (0) 20 7490 9900
www.scalapublishers.com

In association with
The Hepworth Wakefield
Gallery Walk
Wakefield
West Yorkshire
WF1 5AW
www.hepworthwakefield.org

British Library Cataloguing in Publication Data.
A catalogue record for this book is available from
the British Library.

ISBN: 978 1 85759 679 3

Project Manager and Copy Editor: Linda Schofield
Designer: Andrew Shoolbred

Printed and bound in Spain

10 9 8 7 6 5 4 3 2 1

Picture Credits
Front cover and pp.5, 15, 34, 37 (left), 41 (right), 57,
58, 59, 60, 61: photographs © Jonty Wilde; back
cover and pp.1, 9, 11 (bottom), 12, 51, 54, 62–3:
photographs © Iwan Baan; pp.4, 10, 22, 37 (left), 39,
40, 41, 43: all works by Barbara Hepworth © Bowness,
Hepworth Estate; pp.4, 10, 37 (right), 39, 48, 49:
photographs by Norman Taylor; pp.5, 37 (right): repro-
duced by permission of The Henry Moore Foundation;
p.6: Welcome to Yorkshire archive – Photo HD9 Imaging;
p.8 (top): © David Chipperfield Architects (Richard
Davies); pp.8 (bottom), 11 (top), 20–21, 27, 28, 29:
© David Chipperfield Architects; pp.14, 42 (bottom), 44,
45: images courtesy of the Hepworth Estate and photographs © Iwan Baan; pp.17, 30, 33: photographs by
Simon Wallis; pp.19, 42 (top), 46 (left): images courtesy
of the Hepworth Estate and photographs by Studio
St Ives; p.22: photograph courtesy Yorkshire Sculpture
Park © Jonty Wilde; p.25: The British Museum © The
Trustees of the British Museum. All rights reserved; p.26:
photograph by Hannah Webster; pp.40, 43: photographs
by Mark Heathcote, Museum Photography; p.41 (left):
© Tate, London 2011; pp.46 (right), 47: images courtesy
of the Hepworth Estate and photographs by Lucien Myers;
p.48: © The Estate of Patrick Heron. All rights reserved,
DACS, 2011; pp.51, 52, 54, 55: courtesy of Eva
Rothschild and The Hepworth Wakefield; p.52: photograph © Stuart Whipps; p.53: courtesy of Clare Woods
and Stuart Shave Modern Art, London; p.55: photograph
© Jerry Hardman-Jones; p.57: Originally commissioned
by Situations at the University of the West of England
for Victoria Park in Bristol 2009. The commission in
Wakefield is supported by Art in Yorkshire.

All other photographs and artworks: © The Hepworth
Wakefield

Front cover: The Hepworth Wakefield, 2011
Back cover (top): The gallery from the river, 2011
Back cover (bottom): Gallery 6 – Hepworth and
St Ives, 2011
Page 1: The Hepworth Wakefield, footbridge and
River Calder, 2011

**LOTTERY FUNDED**

Supported by
**ARTS COUNCIL ENGLAND**

FOUNDING PARTNERS
Wakefield Council
The Hepworth Estate

MAJOR FUNDERS
Arts Council England
Heritage Lottery Fund

FUNDERS
European Regional Development Fund
Homes and Communities Agency
Yorkshire Forward

MAJOR FUNDERS
Audrey & Stanley Burton Charitable Trust
Garfield Weston Foundation
The Headley Trust
The Wolfson Foundation

DONORS
Esmée Fairbairn Foundation
The Kirby Laing Foundation
Sir George Martin Trust
The Henry Moore Foundation
Lord St Oswald
The Scurrah Wainwright Charity
Sir Siegmund Warburg's Voluntary Settler